still arriving

still arriving

Honorable Mention
of the
2022 Don Gutteridge Poetry Award

Bruce Kauffman

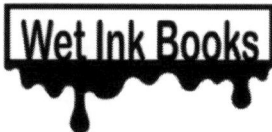

Wet Ink Books

First Edition

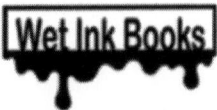

Wet Ink Books
www.WetInkBooks.com
WetInkBooks@gmail.com

Title: still arriving
Author: Bruce Kauffman

Contest Judges: Don Gutteridge, John B. Lee
Cover Photograph: Kelsey Newman Reed
Cover Design: Richard M. Grove
Layout and Design: Richard M. Grove

Typeset in Garamond
Printed and bound in Canada
Distributed in USA by Ingram,
    – to set up an account – 1-800-937-0152

Library and Archives Canada Cataloguing in Publication

Title: Still arriving / Bruce Kauffman.
Names: Kauffman, Bruce, 1950- author.
Description: Poems. | "Honorable mention of the 2022 Don Gutteridge Poetry Award".
Identifiers: Canadiana 20230196985 | ISBN 9781989786819 (softcover)
Classification: LCC PS8621.A685 S75 2023 | DDC C811/.6—dc23

This book is dedicated
to every person and anything
that inspired me
to pick up the pen at all.

Contents:

Late Spring by W. S. Merwin – *p. 1*

– unfinished notes from a journal (# 6) – *p. 3*
– mid-november early morning – *p. 4*
– bridges – *p. 6*
– a crossing in a city – *p. 7*
– watching – *p. 8*
– at the lake – *p. 10*
– autumn – *p. 11*
– telling – *p. 12*
– ferryman – *p. 14*
– proof – *p. 15*
– light – *p. 16*
– an offering – *p. 17*
– having – *p. 18*
– on light again – *p. 19*
– epiphany – *p. 20*
– mourning the day after – *p. 21*
– today – *p. 23*
– another day – *p. 24*
– delicate – *p. 25*
– fluid – *p. 26*
– geese on a grassy ledge – *p. 27*
– in a day – *p. 28*
– difference – *p. 29*
– a nature poet – *p. 30*
– days – *p. 31*
– a portion of a letter to a friend – *p. 32*
– watchmaker – *p. 35*
– then – *p. 36*
– old yellow school bus – p. *37*
– lost in hi-tech – *p. 38*
– Zhivago, again – *p. 39*

– an empty journal – *p. 41*
– who we are – *p. 42*
– unfinished notes from a journal   (# 15) – *p. 43*
– walls – *p. 44*
– before – *p. 45*
– reaching for words – p. *46*
– for 30 days – *p. 47*
– a tree in a forest – *p. 48*
– connected – p. *50*
– gravity – *p. 52*
– gore street – *p. 53*
– gone – *p. 54*
– home – *p. 55*
– morning – *p. 56*
– how – *p. 57*
– reflecting – *p. 58*
– room – *p. 59*
– upon waking – *p. 60*
– sitting here, simply observing – *p. 61*
– returning – *p. 62*
– we – *p. 63*
– outside – *p. 64*
– my words to a park revisited – *p. 65*
– later – *p. 66*
– last whisper – *p. 67*
– the final exit – *p. 68*
– sounds in silence – *p. 70*

About the Author – *p. 73*
Acknowledgement – *p. 74*
Notes – *p. 75*
Front Cover Photographer Bio – *p. 77*

Late Spring

Coming into the high room again after years
after oceans and shadows of hills and the sound of lies
after losses and feet on stairs

after looking and mistakes and forgetting
turning there thinking to find
no one except those I knew
finally I saw you
sitting in white
already waiting

you of whom I had heard
with my own ears since the beginning
for whom more than once
I had opened the door
believing you were not far

W. S. Merwin, from
The Rain in the Trees
(Alfred A. Knopf, 1988)

unfinished notes from a journal (# 6)

July 2019

there is a melancholy rain
outside my window
this evening and
i realize as i write
       that i hold an unguided
       pen in my right hand
its ink as fragile
       as it is indelible

mid-november early morning

morning
slow   quiet this
      sunday morning

this solitary walk back home
a bag of groceries
      at my side
the baggage of a lifetime
      on my shoulders
      back

not another soul
on this sidewalk
      ahead
      or even behind
here in this cold
but not yet bitter wind

here along this, a hollow street on one side
an empty park on the other

across the street
an unpainted wooden deck
and on its rail
      a large white coffee mug
and a same distance
into the park
on its still green grass
      a pink hoodie sweater
      slightly rolled up

either   both
left behind

      mug   sweater

remnants?

or a vanishing?

bridges

bridges left

some set afire by me
        after

others burning
        beneath
as i unknowingly shuffled across

and some already burnt
as i approached but i
crossed still

even then
they nothing more than
        soot and ash
appearing somehow still
as bridge

held together
hanging from the sky
with but the thread
        of an infinite hope

a crossing in a city

as you and i stand
downtown
at an intersection
two main streets crossing

cars   trucks   buses
in all their colours pass by
swarms of pedestrians
in their slow crawl
            on either side

you watch transfixed
by it all
            its flowing colours
            shapes

            and voices

i look at you smiling
embracing it all
and want to tell you
how foreign all of this
            is to me
but cannot

i stand here with
but a language
you have already forgotten

watching

after all these years
after all those years
of always sitting with my back
to the wall
this morning i forgot

or perhaps subconsciously
willed myself to sit in the open
become exposed in it

feeling then completely
vulnerable

but in a quick wave that passes

odd how we discover things
like this

rediscovering openness

finding it now
neither rigid
nor cold

but soft, instead

soft
    like satin
    like a breath

    like a breath   noticed

    like   a first breath   ever

at the lake

i sit here on this side
at water's edge

here in this stillness
pretending to be almost
          silence
whispers break   arrive
from across the lake
gliding just above its water
          an island calls

a calling from a small graveyard there

a calling from another time
a voice
          remembering

autumn

we all
in an autumn
of our days

not simply any autumn
instead perhaps
       that final one

we
on an earth of soil and stone
built our glass cities

and when then for us
glass was not enough
we made them mirror
       and became them

telling

i will tell you
of a unique building
its storefront
  you might like to check
  i say

or i will tell
you about a lost
place in a forest
where two rivers meet
just ahead of the falls
their waters absolutely
   intermingled then

and in the telling
i know already
before the end of day
before even the end of this hour
you will have forgotten

that's understandable
you weren't meant
to remember

it simply wasn't the right time
or place for it

but one day
  weeks
  months
  years
  even decades
from now
you will come
in real life
in happenstance
  if such a thing exists

you will stumble upon
that very unique storefront
or come upon that lost
place in the forest
  and hear the falls nearby

and you will look at either
for a first time

and you will believe
you had never been there
before

but you will recognize it
in a way you cannot understand
  or describe

you will feel a fullness in it
a familiarity you cannot explain

you will call it déjà vu

you will remember it
for the rest of your life

ferryman

quiet comes
the ferryman

the water
before   behind
shows no trace of
ripple   wave

animals   even insects
on this approaching shore
settle
make no sound
as he approaches

this stillness
simply prelude to a coming
longest of silence

it too
          leaving no wake

proof

i write these words
in this journal
        this evening
quite certain they
will go nowhere

i won't share them
won't most likely
ever open this page
or even this filled journal
again

and in more time
i will have forgotten
they were even written

and in more time i may
even misplace this journal
with no way of
rediscovering it and these words
again

yes i am certain
i will misplace them
will lose them
will even forget them

but
i am just as certain it was
infinitely important
that i wrote them

here
        in this place
here
        in this hour

        this evening

light

in the right light
of day
            and self
even wall
becomes
            mirage

an offering

not prayer

simpler
        perhaps

a statement
request
a word of thanks

to god   or gods
energy   or universe
to a wavering agnostic belief

to that spirit of endless time
          without time

to the known
the unknowing
the unknowable

to softness
in a world of too little of it

having

it having heard
in a whispered sleep

stories of rain
peppered with sun

a green day
       comes

on light again

a seldom remembered
fact about light

if reflected
often times is
twice
       as bright

epiphany

for this poet
      this late in life

a reminder that
lesser writ
those morning and vibrant poems
      of youth
instead now
these evening and mourning poems
of and to
      the dead
      the dying

mourning the day after

for W. S. Merwin

i

having learned late
last night of your death

this morning
the mourning begins

i leave my house early

walk partway through town
to my favourite small quiet café

dressed in black
        to become invisible

casual clothes   loose-fitting
hiding structure and bone
        to forget

no conversation
needed   wanted

just the motion
this movement
around me
to remember
there still is

        you
        my favourite poet

        you
        who made me fall
        in love
                with poetry

you
  still active in it
  even at 91

as you sat that last day in your garden
perhaps laying down an
        unfinished line on a page
then in that instant took the rest
with you as you disappeared

ii

and now
you are out of sight but
        somewhere yet
your voice   your words
behind me
        i still hear

and i still here   this morning
attempting poetry
with my but awkward child-hands
my coloured crayons between
clumsy fingers and ungraceful thumb
scribbling injured and splintered words
in crooked   broken lines
on a journal's page
        for as long as it takes

See Note 1

today

we are ever-residing in a moment
with future and past
    running wild through us

See Note 2

another day

billowy clouds
loosening
narrowing   thinning

throwing out slender
fingers of themselves
reaching
seeming haphazard
but instead prescribed
        directed
        attached

to a deeper blue sky
they stretch their patterns

i watch
reading their global messages
        like tea leaves in a cup

delicate

how delicate life is

how time moves in it
with its always still
one thing gentle

even this morning

over there
under a wall's wooden ledge

an empty broken   brittle
split   shell of a cocoon
in an early morning breeze

it swirling   twirling
still moving   swaying
dancing
to its own
and only   ever-song

fluid

at the mouth of a river
a grand lake watches
its water leaving

a lake
in its fluid wonder
          memory
fears its best
parts are moving on
while a river
with its now new
fingers   knees
crawls away

with its new eyes
sees what lake
can never see

a river
calling back
    these new places
    stories to tell

and a lake
    no longer able to hear

geese on a grassy ledge

at the very edge of a lake
just above in its short grass
      on a ledge
three mother geese
stand fully upright   erect
long necks stretched
constantly turning back
      and forth
ever on guard

their endless watch
for any thing
in any direction

interspersed between them
their fourteen goslings
heads down   foraging
oblivious to anything external
focused only on feeding
their bills in the grass
and small flowers at their feet

it is more than duty
these elders so closely watch

it is equal parts
a mother's love and caring
and an instinctual
      whispered drive deeper
protecting not only day
or family
      but species as well

in a day

in a day it will be over

in 24 hours
you will be standing
or sitting still
in this very spot
and unbeknownst to you
everything you know
will have been undone

you will not notice
even one in an infinitude of
incremental changes
in each and every thing

we barely realize surface
never fully recognize
how absolute is process

and in it all
how quickly
          time moves

how slow
          the evolution

difference

of profound difference

asked to sit and
when prompted then to
either create a poem
or allow one

opt for the latter

and there
become not the poet
instead
the ink
       the page

a nature poet

i am a nature poet
         i guess

simply spending my days now
collecting feathers
polishing stones

days

at day's end
yet another numeric sheet
from a page-a-day calendar
falls leaflike
from desk to floor

it there finding its truest
purpose
being swept then
into that night's fireplace

and when lit by a match
beneath a bundle of wood
becomes the next morning's fire

a portion of a letter to a friend

... did something a bit unusual yesterday
i have to say that i am impulsive.

having noticed the box of miniature christmas lights in the back
corner of my closet
very early yesterday morning (like when i got up),
and in it realized i hadn't really noticed them in many years –
    have had that unopened box of them at least 2 decades,
    maybe more,

when i went to metro a couple of hours later and
noticed the small xmas trees there –
    thought about the lights again.

coming back from cfrc yesterday, about noon,
i cut through metro's parking lot having come up division.
saw the trees again,
    went inside to ask about them –

and yeah, you saw this coming, ended up picking one up.
brought it home, it's only like 3 feet tall maybe –
    so perfect size
    and the only reason i even considered it –

cut the cellophane from the box and unravelled the lights
& strung them around the tree immediately after getting home,
    which btw fit perfectly, and so as i did the full
afternoon and evening yesterday, i now sit with it, lights on - just off
to my left this morning.

i haven't owned a tree since maybe december of the year 2000.
when i was married
and a couple of years after (2 christmases) i lived with a family here
and that anyway being their tree, not mine – and that
sort of 'thing' then was their joy, not so much my own –

but i can confess, it did bring a warmth to the cold winter season
and here i am now with something i'd vowed for years
i would never have in my home again. and i don't know why —
but it just seemed the thing to do this year.

perhaps a small comfort in the craziness outside.

i was always spiritual —
        but i really stopped short of saying the word 'god' - or esp 'God' —
that spiritual recognition was always attributed
        in my thoughts and language as
        'the universe', 'nature', 'truth'.
but for the last couple of years, even before the pandemic
        i found and now find myself
using the words god - and god to mean the all of it.
        and not the angry god of old testament stuff,
        but the benevolent one.
and i am not studied enough in it to know
all the versions of all the christian variations,
or even more all the varied religions of the world
but this god i mention, like a tree - i need to know nothing about.
it's not important that i know. but what is important though is
that it is there, like a tree, for shade in the heat, for shelter in a storm.

odd thing here,
in my apartment — alone —— just now - as i was typing that last line —
the lamp behind me turned on — and i am now sitting here even
more humble and a bit overwhelmed. it is a very peaceful feeling.

i was reminded of long ago how Arlo Guthrie's song
'Valley to Pray / Gabriel's Mother's Hiway Ballad No. 16 Blues'
contained the repeated line of 'come on children come on' —
in fact, i believed it to be the title   but more relevant
i am told that he said after, once, in an interview that when he was
composing the song one afternoon and

as he was sitting at his piano and singing with it
the words again 'come on children come on.
All God's children...'
there on an altogether cloudy day, in an instant,
the clouds broke for a few seconds and a crack of light
slid through his window and shone across the keys of his piano

so you see —
i have watched myself and looking back now
allowed those years of cynicism,
to become years of atheism,
then agnosticism, then at least now
has become that of a somewhat reluctant,
but still more than just simple, acceptance.

and, yeah, don't know - don't even know why
i thought it was important to let you know —

but yeah - don't read more into all this than it is —
i'm still trying to figure it out myself —

i hope you are well, my friend,

and i hope you have a wonderful and peaceful day ...

all best, ...

watchmaker

the old watchmaker
at the end
of this narrow street
this morning
looks up
      from his own
removes his glasses

lays down
his loupe
his miniature tools

slides back
trays of
      springs and gears
      metal arms   hands
      dots and numbers
      bands   chains
      crystals and pins
as he gazes
through his open door
      transfixed
with a morning's
sky   fields   trees
beyond his desk then street

and this late
      this morning
after a full life
of perfecting time
realizes for the first time
      its illusion

then

i refuse to go back now
to those places of my youth

there in its only self ascribed
brilliant light
to find it simply
faded   jaded

to find as well
in every building
on every floor
behind every door
and on its pathways to
and pastures from
nothing but
ghost and shadow

skeletons masquerading
as something else

this land of still wanting to be
something finished
something more

becomes this land empty
nothing here but echo
mid-sentence
          ever-dying

old yellow school bus

perhaps more humility
than economy
and without a
limo'd pretentiousness
an old yellow
school bus approaches

a sheet of white typing paper
taped to the bottom of
its front windshield
near the door

and hand-printed in
bold black ink
with letters large enough
to be easily seen
by anyone even twenty feet away

were simply these words:
        "MacMillan Wedding Party"

lost in high tech

in a time when things were
done more slowly
expectation was less

immediacy then not yet a word

there was an intimacy
back then
in a search
   in a library
   at a small store
those casual unplanned crossings
of paths conversations
friendships began

those days had fewer sharp edges

we are now replacing
the flesh of all things
with digitization monitor
holograph endless screen
they nothing but surface
all without
the warmth of a gentle
    blood pulsing beneath

Zhivago, again

After Boris Pasternak's novel, "Doctor Zhivago",
with reference to a scene in David Lean's 1965 film
based on the book.

oh, Pasternak
        Zhivago
how you arrive again
in these days
and my dreams
to comfort   to haunt

we both   all
torn inside   outside
by family   place

yours and my
        fiction or not
different era-ed
distant but somehow
        parallel lives
either of us married to ink
as much as flesh

and this morning
dear Larissa
after I now too
have become
        the deserter
having crossed through blizzards
over frozen tundra
left my steed dead
        along the way

then stumbling
        almost frozen
find myself
as if surprised at last to be
at the foot of your building
with snow/wind-burnt eyes
looking up the stairs
to the door of your flat
fumble with a loosened stone
        a secret place in the wall
to find your key   and a note to me
saying *What joy!!*   *I've heard you*
have been spotted just outside of town
I am so excited to learn you are
both still alive   *and here*

and i stand here trembling
as i read it this morning
nearly frozen
nearly dead
        almost home

an empty journal

in an overcrowded café

i reach into my knapsack
pull out this new journal
crack its spine open
the first time

it is as new as this day

while this day   today
only appears to be
a photocopy   carbon copy
of all the days before

this day instead
unique   one
in all lifetimes

and it too
as crystalline

       as its memory
       soon will be

who we are

there are ghosts
in my writings

nothing that might be
noticed   or missed

the slightest clipping
of hair   just a quarter inch

or a half-thimble full
of exhaled breath

an idea of shadow

and these still
in and of themselves
revealing more
of ghost   of them
or you   or us

        than even history
        or dna

unfinished notes from a journal   (# 15)

no one, really, writes
letters anymore

i don't know
if that makes these special
or simply old fashioned
        archaic

these notes have no intention
        really
of anything
they are each simply
a superficial glimpse
surface
        a piece of place
        and time

an idea i cling to here
is that
        at least for me
it is a fallacy
that age brings wisdom

perhaps someone more rigid
in their beliefs would
not feel the same

you will find no answers
in these letters
nor will you find advice

you might though find in them
a single word or a phrase
you can carry with you
to discover your own wisdom
in another place

walls

as if a wall
partitioning the outside
from the in
       wasn't enough
you built an extra layer
added an additional
       another wall

and now you can't hear
anything behind it
       on either side
and you wonder

why you
       can no longer feel

before

...a full day before
the loud rumble everyone else heard
resonating from kilometers in the distance
beneath ocean's floor
there then earth plates shifting

and here dinner plates rattling
with teacups in cupboards
artwork, books, and hung pictures falling
to a shaking floor

...and still a half-day before

the tsunami waves hit
leveling villages
deep-sea burying and washing away
people, animals, trees, and farms

there you sat in silence
on that same beach
and watched a static
glass ocean's surface

and there right before you
as if from nothing
as if hesitating
a slightest
            single ripple
                        formed

reaching for words

for Allison Chisholm

i'm trying to write poetry
sitting in a small café that has
3 kinds of coffee
10 different pastries
but only 17 words

and a poet at another table
has already used
10 of them

for 30 days

make a commitment
to write a short poem
            a day
and after seven days
double it

and make it happen

better still -
            simply know it will

do not feel anxious
when you begin each day
do not feel guilty
on an evening you've failed

but do it still
for 30 days

and on the 31st
call me   tell me
how much
            your life has changed

a tree in a forest

a lone tree   standing
on the side of a large hill
ruggedly   reluctantly
remembering others
            once

remembering five years ago
    in a morning just like all the rest
    coming then mid-day
first a rushing of powerful wind
and then an impossible heat

a tree learning that day
new words in its language
        fire   forest fire

a tree remembering how that raged
until all others   were gone
it left standing in a smoky haze
with but wound and scar
of 2 blackened bottom branches

lost its leaves off those that year
            again the next four
does not yet fully understand
they will never grow back

and here it stands feeling
lucky   and lost
but waking today to a morning
its mild dewy breeze

this new morning of forgiving sun
here the fourth spring after
this tree watching and upon waking
seeing on this expanse
of short grass and wildflowers
hundreds of new
tree seedlings and saplings
glistening on a hill

with then a hill remembering
itself again

connected

for Meg Freer, after her reading at Poets @ Artfest viii, July 1, 2022

at a poetry festival
a poet was reading at the mic

that poet well connected to nature
walking daily   hiking
taking photos of it

and as i moved just behind the audience
listening to her reading
a crow landed in the tree beside me

sat on its lowest branch
just above my head
a branch i could almost reach
and touch with outstretched arm

as i listened i looked up at the crow
and looked straight into its eyes

she was watching the poet
and let out the softest
sweetest caw i had ever heard

i assumed it might be the only one

but after a short pause
another softest of caws again
then another pause
another soft caw

this happened nine times

from the poet's daily outings
did the crow recognize
her?

was it merely as if greeting
a comrade   a friend?

or was the crow
appreciating the sound
the quality   or message
of the poem and letting us know

i'll have to ask the next time
i see her

next time i see
        the poet

        or the crow

gravity

you will ever-arrive
in those times when
you fully sense
that even gravity is
    porous

gore street

sunday evenings
the best evenings really
      downtown

always fewer people

a quieter tone
a mellower energy

and it always best at that time of day
with the sun almost ready to set
in its dusk coloured sky

this evening -
a planned walk that would end with
city park and queen's university campus
on my return home

but first downtown
it was all perfect
walked down queen to king st east
walked up to and then thru market square
saw someone i knew in the distance
and waved a 'hello'
walked down to ontario street and then out to gore

i love that very short street for some reason
perhaps because a very dear friend, sarah,
once lived there a couple of years before
      she moved away
and i've known three other friends
who had lived on it as well

maybe i so love it too because it
doesn't really go anywhere

three or four blocks
it's there
      and then it's not

gone

this morning i packed up
the few things left of you
in a box

and placed it in a spot
       our favourite spot
for those even dearer to you
to pick up

you were here
for such a short time, really
and now in the bleakness
of an empty space
waiting for words to fill
i have none

you who were here
one moment
your face radiant
arms always moving
       as you talked
looking at me
       straight in my eyes and
in an instant
       after
you

gone

this all still so early

as if that first day
in the drought
       of a lifetime

       a last morning dew

home

living alone these past
fifteen years

long ago befriended in it
the quietness

spoke even then of
      the different notes
      and arrangements
in that
      music of silence

and always in that time
have chosen the aloneness

the smallest of apartments
in which to dwell

i do think perhaps
i had always the heart
of a gypsy

but just never
      the feather

      the wing

morning

morning will pass
itself into afternoon

wearing then only
its fading paint
and thinner skin

knowing still
            though
it will have forgotten
            nothing

how

funny how time is

one day we're lost in
daredevil stunts
miming immortality
scoffing at an absurd idea
       of becoming old

and then
next thing you know
it's thirty   forty
years on and

in an instant
we've become it

reflecting

i know only for certain
that to a weary eye
in the night
even a flashlight
becomes the moon

room

this room in an old limestone
university building
no longer knows itself

new windows
new carpet
paint
new shiny baseboards
       and trim

all of this hides its bones
its skeleton walls

there are whispers
behind the paint

whispers confused
can't understand why
they are no longer flesh

their skeleton-memories
lucid   reborn
in whisper so soft
not intending to haunt
but to simply remind

another time
other lives
      once as real as this

once as real
     as yours

once as real
     as you

upon waking

realized
not with all days   but still
sometimes one
          so polished
with a smoothest of slowness
and the feel of it so full
that a handful of it after
rests unused on
          your nightstand
to slide into your dreams

sitting here, simply observing

i have been sitting
in this park for
nearly twenty years
waiting
            for something

            to arrive

nothing comes
            nothing changes

people   things
move
beside me
around me
always but
            only flicker
            shadow

none of it with even a bit
            of heartbeat still

and then in an instant
a profound sense of entanglement
quantum
            moves into

            then through

returning

for kelly

to see a ghost
from the past
      this early morning

it as real
      as the day

both her   and it
silent
      sitting
      growing
          new flesh

we

we
like a flowering plant

there are those seeming forever times
where we are and must simply be
both an ugly stem absorbing and
an invisible tenuous and thirsty root
taking in that sun and moon above
the water and soil beneath

we
all of this
           before the flower comes

outside

i sit on a bench outside
ghosts
linger

they put on
another face
camouflage a voice

a bird behind me
pecks once at a metal windowpane
hesitates one full second
and then pecks again
hesitates   and then again
and again   and again
            mimics footsteps
                      heartbeat

i realize now that
to say "ghosts linger"
is but half truth

to use those words
suggests something once
has left   is lost

what if leaving
or reluctance to
are the parts that
aren't true

what if

all of whatever once was
            still is
alive today
if we could
            only see

my words to a park revisited

to you park,

whispered secrets shared with you
twenty years ago kept both then and now
could only mean we must still be friends

coming back on you now for again
the first in all this time   though
i am afraid i have to say
how much you've aged

branches lost
even full trees felled

some of those mid sized then
i do not recognize now

and these smaller trees
i remember even less

i thought i knew you well

i thought i knew you better

just noticing now
i am quite certain
this reflecting pond
sitting on your west side
was not there back then

and i am quite certain, as well,
that on this pond's surface
i know neither the face
nor the old man looking back at me
as I look into
         and through

later

before these years of canes
there were days and nights
of dance   forest hikes

this old man walking here now
his ungainly stroll and in his mind
again today memories roll
a time long ago   before even any of this
that first time
his tiny hands on a short coffee table   found
from that expanded crawl
his head stretching above
standing full up his eyes barely seeing over the top
both hands take full hold   wobbly knees
then something across the room
catches his eye   he lets go his grip
takes a step   his first
becoming then a lifetime of them

and he now
eighty years on
a slight tremor in his hand
a hesitation in his breath

this more common fear
        of falling

and an even more pressing fear now
perhaps having to relearn
        how to crawl

last whisper

a whisper
still resting on a tongue
       cold
lips sealed
       rigid

those last whispers
we take with us
as we leave…

never having had a chance
to settle on their intended ears

these secrets
only the embalmer
and mortician
       hear

the final exit

i'd like to believe
that when we leave
     this world
we do it without
breaking stride
     or even rise from
       where we were
and continue to walk
that next step through
     a most delicate of veil

and as it gently brushes
across each our face
over our head
and down our back
it dusts clean
the whole of pain and regret
ever worn in our lives

and we then with a very
clearest of eye   and vision
look straight ahead to see
the grandest of a city park
     almost forest before us
with the longest
of clear pathway through

we walk and watch in an
easy twilight
        an ever-dusk
with a coolest of breeze
washing across our face
on a lukewarm
        as if summer evening and
everywhere but ahead
there is an ultimate and
profound silence

and straight ahead on this
path that goes on
        forever
that only sound
seeming always just beyond

a lone encouraging but still
melancholy mandolin
gently directing
calling us
farther and
farther into
        and through

sounds in silence

a shout will last as long
as its own voice and breath
in that instant will allow

might even travel
as far as some distant
canyon wall

and then bounce back
once   or twice
again

a whisper though
travels below it all

goes on
            forever

About the Author

Bruce Kauffman lives in Kingston, Ontario and is a local poet, editor, and organizer of literary events. His written work has appeared in several anthologies and journals, two chapbooks, and four collections of poetry, with still arriving his fifth. Beyond writing and editing, he facilitates intuitive writing workshops. In 2009 he founded, and still organizes and hosts the monthly 'and the journey continues' open mic reading series. In 2010 he debuted his weekly spoken word radio show, 'finding a voice', on CFRC 101.9fm, and continues to produce and host it. You can find him on Facebook. Email: bruce.kauffman@hotmail.com

Acknowledgement

mid-november early morning – *p. 4*
A variation of this poem was prev. published in the Winter 2020/21 Issue of Devour: Art & Lit Canada

Watching – *p. 8*
Previously published in the Winter 2021/22 Issue of Devour: Art & Lit Canada

delicate – *p. 25*
Previously published in the "Inspired Heart forTeens: Identity and Diversity" anthology (Melinda Cochrane Inspired Books, 2021)

a portion of a letter to a friend – *p. 32*
Previously published in the "Inspired Heart for Teens: Identity and Diversity" anthology (Melinda Cochrane Inspired Books, 2021)

before – *p. 45*
Previously published in Ultraviolet Review 02/16/20

a tree in a forest – *p. 48*
Previously published in Skeleton Press - June 2022

gone – *p. 54*
A variation of this poem was previously published in the Summer 2020 Issue of Devour: Art & Lit Canada

home – *p. 55*
Previously published in the Summer 2020 Issue of Devour: Art & Lit Canada. And a version of it on Artfest Kingston's Poetry website.

upon waking – *p. 60*
A variation of this poem was previously published in the Summer 2022 Issue of Devour: Art & Lit Canada

sitting here, simply observing – *p. 61*
A variation of this poem was previously published in Ultraviolet Magazine - 2020/21

outside – *p. 64*
A variation of this poem was previously published in the Summer 2022 Issue of Devour: Art & Lit Canada

my words to a park revisited – *p. 65*
A variation of this poem was Previously published in the Winter 2020/21 Issue of Devour: Art & Lit Canada

Notes

1) W. S. Merwin was born on September 30, 1927 and died March 15, 2019. Over the course of his life, he wrote over 50 books of poetry or prose, produced many works of translation, and among numerous other honours he was twice-awarded a Pulitzer Prize for Poetry. He was named the Poet Laureate of the United States in 2010.

What follows here are my more personal observations about him. Although I'd already been writing poetry for over twenty years then, I did not come across his writings until the very early to mid 1990's. It was a sunny afternoon in a very large three-story bookstore with huge windows. On the third floor, the store had many massive bookshelves filled with books of poetry.

I was pulling several poet's collections down, one at a time, looking for those whose work I could easily relate to. I did find some. Jotted down those names, but still put all their books back in their correct spots on the shelves.

I'd already been looking through them for over an hour that day, when finally, I found several books by someone named W. S. Merwin. I pulled down, first, his The Rain in the Trees. I read the first poem in it. I was awestruck, I couldn't put it down. I leaned against the bookcase and leafed through that book, reading page after page. Fully engrossed.

It was like I'd found a lost language, but I understood it. There, filled with wonder, I was as if retraining myself to decipher and navigate that language. I believe I was finally in it all able to discover the poet in myself, as well.

After reading at least fifteen poems in The Rain in the Trees, I put it on a small table beside me as if to claim the book. I found another of his that enticed me. Spent much time with it. And then another. And another. Finally, having well-leafed through yet another, I collected his Second Four Books of Poems, placed it on the small table with the other, as if taking a mental snapshot for an instant, and then gathered them and headed to the cashier to pay for them both.

To date, I have acquired over a dozen of his books. All displayed on a shelf in a bookcase in my apartment. I love them all, but it is his first book mentioned here, that I absolutely do still love the most.

I felt it incredibly important in this collection to include, along with my elegiac poem 'mourning the day after', to also include on an opening page, as an epigraph - that very first poem of his I read that day in the store.

He, remains, for me, the most positive of proof that a poet can completely change another person's life. He did mine.

2)   The poem, 'today', first appeared not in a publication, but still in print. It was part of a series of poet/visual artist collaborations that covered a billboard at a busy intersection in what is known as "The Hub" here. The project was envisioned by the City of Kingston. As with another poet before me (Kingston Poet Laureate Jason Heroux), and then one after me (Chantel Lavoie), the artistic layouts for each of our very short poems was interpreted by an artist who then laid out the billboard - and those, again, did hang at that busy intersection for a three to four month period. My poem was displayed March - June, 2021. You can find much more information about that project on the City of Kingston's website (link below), but from it, as a lead-in: "The Hub Project is a multi-phase initiative designed to connect neighbourhoods through art by making a series of temporary and permanent improvements to the intersection of Princess and Division streets, known as 'The Hub'…"
Here's the full link: https://www.cityofkingston.ca/city-hall/projects-construction/the-hub-project

Front Cover Photographer

Kelsey Newman Reed is an artist, published poet, and has always been passionate about the arts. She has spent many years crafting poems and illustrations that tell stories of the trees, the moon, (our) hands, and the water. If she isn't able to write about nature or draw it, Kelsey will often spend time taking photos of the shadows the sun makes, and how the plants dance within it. Her work often attempts to feel serene, calm, and soft.